LONDON
from the air

PHOTOGRAPHED BY Ian Hay, Flight Images
TEXT BY Lisa Pritchard

MYRIAD
LONDON

Title page: St James's Park and Whitehall;
this page: the Thames winds through London

ISBN 1 904 154 35 2

Designed by Jerry Goldie Graphic Design
Printed in China

www.myriadbooks.com

Contents

Introduction

Stand on a street-corner today in central London: watch the people go by and listen to the multitude of languages. It is as if the world has come to the British capital. This is a truly cosmopolitan city – for centuries successive generations of migrants have enriched its cultural and commercial life.

The Thames is London's birth mother: the curve of a slow-flowing tidal river with easy access to the sea was a natural place for the invading Romans to build a settlement in AD43. The broad river and its marshy banks had previously held invaders at bay, but in the years that followed it became an important artery for the empire's seaborne trade in slaves, animal skins, cattle, grain, iron and precious metals. Today the international commercial hub known as the City of London is still bounded by fragments of the Roman city wall.

The City built up its trading credentials through the Middle Ages. As new communities sprang up, they built churches: London had more than any other European city of that era. Four centuries later the Saxon king Edward the Confessor made Westminster the seat of national government and ordered the transformation of Westminster Abbey. He set the scene for the creative tension that has existed ever since between the trade-based culture of the City and the legislative authority of Westminster.

In 1665 an outbreak of bubonic plague tore through the overcrowded housing, killing 68,950 people – one-fifth of London's population. The following year the Great Fire of London destroyed a great swathe of the city, including St Paul's Cathedral, 87 churches and 13,200 houses. Miraculously only about a dozen people died. In the years that followed Sir Christopher Wren was charged with rebuilding the city.

London's steady expansion has absorbed surrounding towns and villages to an extent that may surprise today's residents. In the latter part of the 17th century, Kensington was considered a country retreat well away from the unhealthy air and filth of central London.

The technological advances of the Industrial Revolution in the 18th and 19th centuries brought huge economic and social change. The mist and fog that had characterised London periodically combined with ever-increasing air pollution to form a noxious smog. After 12,000 people died during the winter of 1952 clean air laws were enacted, and now the hackneyed images of London's landmarks emerging from a pea-souper are no longer reality.

Today's residents and visitors see this great historical legacy of fabulous and quirky buildings from ground level or perhaps from thousands of feet up as they fly in to Heathrow. From a bird's eye view, as in this book, unfamiliar perspectives emerge.

Much of London is not manicured perfection, but a haphazard mix of old and new. Alongside tiny family-run cafes and fish and chip shops, bingo halls, shopping malls and high-rise housing, modern London offers vibrant culture, world-renowned universities, stunning restaurants, fabulous shopping and outstanding modern working environments.

This is a dynamic city. More than 200 years later Dr Samuel Johnson's declaration still holds true: "When a man is tired of London he is tired of life; for there is in London all that life can afford."

Lisa Pritchard

London, old and new: from Greenwich to the Isle of Dogs

The West End

FOR MOST VISITORS, the West End is London: its combination of shopping, culture, history and nightlife are an almost irresistible lure and many feel that this part of the capital offers everything they need. For Londoners the term implies everything upmarket, from housing to department stores, theatres and restaurants.

Beyond the well-trodden tourist trail is a fascinating patchwork of everyday life. Real people live out their lives, children go to school, adults make their way to work and take their children to the park.

Historically, the West End sprang up as London grew richer and more confident, expanding into the fields and villages to the west of the City of London. That confidence remains the hallmark of the area today.

Westminster *above* and Hyde Park, bordered by Park Lane *right*

PARLIAMENT *(above)*

The Gothic splendour of the House of Commons, and its upper house, the Lords, is more recent than one might imagine. After fire ravaged much of the old Palace of Westminster in 1834, Charles Barry designed Parliament's new home in keeping with the Gothic masterpiece of Westminster Abbey, seen here in the foreground. The Commons was again destroyed during the Second World War, by an incendiary bomb, and rebuilt according to Barry's original design.

BIG BEN *(left)*

This universally recognised symbol of London is named after the huge 13-tonne bell that hangs inside and strikes the hours. The chimes have been broadcast by the BBC since New Year's Eve in 1923. When a bomb struck the Commons in 1941, the tower was unscathed and the chimes of Big Ben remained a powerful symbol of steadfastness to all who heard them. When Parliament is in session a light shines above the clock faces. All four faces are illuminated at night. Each one is some 23ft (7m) square, and the minute hands are over 15ft (4.5m) long. The clock's timekeeping is precisely regulated with old penny pieces to adjust the arc of the giant pendulum.

WESTMINSTER ABBEY (right)

The Abbey has witnessed great moments in British history since Henry III decided to build a cathedral on the site of Edward the Confessor's original abbey. Down the centuries, monarchs have been crowned and married here. Many are also buried in the Abbey, as are others who have had an impact on the nation's cultural and political life. Poets' Corner includes the Elizabethan poet Ben Jonson, buried standing up in a tiny plot just two feet square. Another tomb commemorates Thomas Parr who apparently died at the age of 152. Research indicates three generations of Parrs bore the same name and lived in the same village, so the birth date of 1483 quoted may have been his grandfather's.

PALACE OF WESTMINSTER (below)

From the mid-11th century to 1512 the Palace of Westminster on the banks of the Thames served as a royal residence and focal point for the court. Today the Queen visits just once a year for the State Opening of Parliament. The palace's 1,200 rooms (and over 2 miles of corridors) include the House of Commons, the House of Lords and the octagonal Central Lobby, where members of the public can meet their MPs.

DOWNING STREET *(right)*

The familiar sight of the door of 10 Downing Street, the official residence of the Prime Minister since 1735, is just visible to visitors through the wrought iron gates installed for added security at the Whitehall end of the street. The original 17th century terrace of private houses was built on the site of a brewery, when Number 10 started out as Number 5. The last private resident of Number 10 was named Mr Chicken. Today just three of the houses remain. Numbers 11 and 12 are the homes of the Chancellor of the Exchequer and the Government's Chief Whip respectively.

FOREIGN AND COMMONWEALTH OFFICE *(below)*

With the expansion of the British Empire throughout the 18th and 19th centuries, the role of the Foreign Office grew in importance and its accommodation expanded from one to several houses in Downing Street. At this time the area was very busy, with street traders, lodgings and private houses mixed in with departments of state, dressmakers and livery stables. But as the ground was quite boggy, in the 1860s the site was cleared and foundations sunk for new buildings (collectively known as Whitehall) designed by George Gilbert Scott to house four separate ministries. Today the whole complex is occupied by the Foreign and Commonwealth Office.

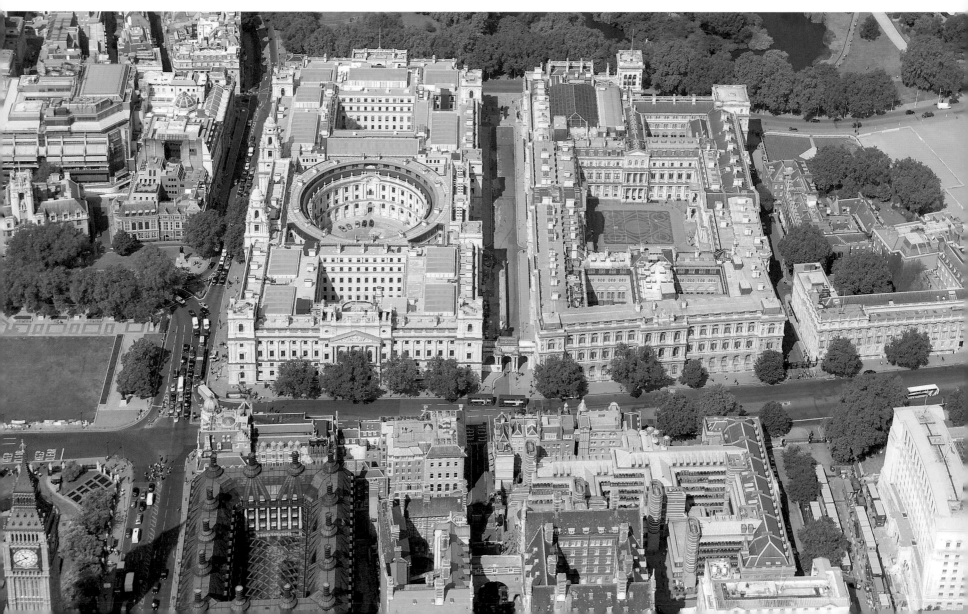

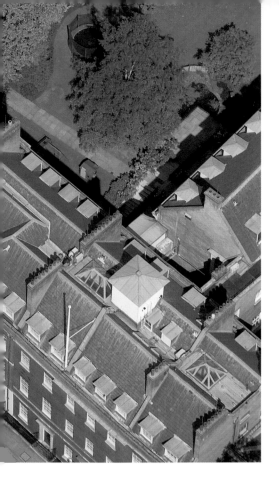

WHITEHALL PLACE (above)

To reach the river from the top of the Mall you can either walk along leafy Northumberland Avenue (right of picture) or after a short detour down Whitehall, you can walk down Whitehall Place (centre). Tucked between the two is Great Scotland Yard. In 1839, two police commissioners set up offices in Whitehall Place to organise the new Metropolitan Police Force, with a police station to the rear that became known as Scotland Yard.

PORTCULLIS HOUSE (left)

This purpose-built office block for MPs was opened by the Queen in 2001 after years of controversy. It was commissioned in 1992 at a cost of £165m, but as the building costs soared and were compounded by delays, the final cost reached £235m. Four floors are occupied by MPs and their staff, while three further floors house Select Committee Rooms, meeting rooms, television interview studios, a vote office and e-library. There are few if any conventional clocks in the building: all computers, phones and the closed circuit annunciator screens display the time.

The energy efficient design of the building means it uses about one-third of the fuel for a comparable building with conventional air conditioning. Fig trees provide shade in the courtyard and reduce the need for cooling in the summer.

WHITEHALL *(left)*

Running from Trafalgar Square to Westminster Bridge, Whitehall is both intensely political and steeped in ceremonial traditions. Key government offices are on either side. The white neoclassical Main Building houses the Ministry of Defence, as well as a remarkable Tudor wine cellar, dating from the original Whitehall Palace. Downing Street, just below Horseguards Parade, is rather dwarfed by the imposing classical lines of the Foreign and Commonwealth Office, with its central courtyard.

In November the Cenotaph in Whitehall is the focus for the annual commemoration of those who died in the two world wars and later conflicts. The royal family and political leaders lay wreaths and war veterans march past to pay their respects.

HORSEGUARDS PARADE

Horseguards was once the headquarters of the British Army. It is named after the mounted troops who have traditionally guarded the monarch since Charles II. Before 1841 the Mall was closed off, and this was the official entrance to St James's and Buckingham Palace. Only those with an Ivory Pass from the Queen are entitled to ride or drive along Horseguards, on the perimeter of St James's Park.

The great rectangle of the parade ground used to be Henry VIII's tilt-yard, where knights would have jousted in front of the Palace of Whitehall. Rather less glamorously in modern times it was used as a car park for civil servants until the 1990s.

Most people will best know Horseguards Parade for the matchless ceremony of Trooping the Colour that marks the Queen's official birthday every June. The ceremony originated with the daily parading of each regiment's flag (colour) before the troops to ensure that they would recognise it in the heat of battle. June also sees the massed bands of the Household Division perform the spectacular Beating Retreat on Horseguards Parade.

ADMIRALTY ARCH

Admiralty Arch succeeds in insulating the Mall from the hectic swirl of Trafalgar Square. The triple arch at its centre is the ceremonial entrance to the Mall and Buckingham Palace. It was built in 1910 in memory of Queen Victoria, as offices for Royal Navy chiefs.

13

BUCKINGHAM PALACE

A perennial favourite, Buckingham Palace is on the list of buildings you must see when you visit London for the first time. It was in fact Queen Victoria who decided to make it her main residence and subsequent monarchs have followed her tradition.

This is more than just a royal residence, however: it is in effect the administrative heart of the monarchy. The palace houses the offices of the Royal Household that supports the activities of the Queen and her immediate family. The need for such a large staff becomes apparent as every year the palace hosts more than 50,000 guests, attending banquets, lunches, dinners, receptions and royal garden parties.

The ceremony of Changing the Guard takes place daily during the summer (every other day in winter) at 11.30am, unless the weather is very wet. For most of the year these are serving soldiers from the Household Division, who see active military duty in addition to this traditional posting. The new Guard marches with a band from Wellington Barracks to the palace forecourt where they ceremonially take over guard duty from the sentries.

VICTORIA MEMORIAL
(right)

Buckingham Palace is set at the end of the Mall, a grand avenue designed by Charles II. As you approach the palace along this broad, tree-lined boulevard you see the palace's imposing facade at its best. In front of the palace stands the Victoria Memorial, built in 1911 to commemorate the 63 years of Queen Victoria's reign from 1837-1901. In June 2002, a million people crowded all approaches to Buckingham Palace, the Mall, Trafalgar Square, the parks and beyond, to celebrate Queen Elizabeth II's golden jubilee.

In the picture (left) you can clearly see the glorious greenery of the gardens behind the palace, while the leafy expanse of Green Park unfolds to the left of the Victoria Memorial. On the right-hand side of the Mall the parkland continues with St James's Park. Until 1904 people could buy fresh milk from cows tethered at the far end of this park, a spot now dominated by Admiralty Arch, as the Mall leads into Trafalgar Square.

VICTORIA

Just a few blocks away from Buckingham Palace, bustling Victoria station (right) serves the southern commuter areas and the south coast. In the days when train travel was seen as rather more glamorous than it is today, posters advertised the station as the "gateway to the Continent". This was the starting point for adventures on the Orient Express in its heyday. Today Victoria is a major transport hub with overground and underground stations as well as the nearby coach station.

At the Parliament Square end of Victoria Street stands Westminster Abbey. Near to the station is Westminster Cathedral, the foremost Roman Catholic church in England and Wales. Inspired by the neo-Byzantine style of St Mark's in Venice and St Vitale in Ravenna, the cathedral's warm tones stand out from the surrounding grey.

NEW SCOTLAND YARD *(below)*

The revolving triangular sign in front of New Scotland Yard is a familiar sight to television viewers. The building is the headquarters of the London Metropolitan Police, but the everyday use of the name Scotland Yard has come to mean one particular branch, the Criminal Investigation Department (CID).

Sir Robert Peel established the Metropolitan Police Force in 1829, and the first

officers were known as Peelers. Today the Metropolitan Police is responsible not only for policing Greater London but also for national and international police work, such as counter-terrorism. The City of London, the square mile at the heart of the capital, has its own police force.

TATE BRITAIN

This pillar of the art establishment for the last hundred years could be said to be built on sugar. Henry Tate started as a grocer's apprentice but saw the potential of a new sugar refining technique. He also introduced the sugar lump to Britain and went on to make his fortune. He gave his remarkable art collection to the nation, and paid for the building of a gallery on Millbank to house it. The collection today focuses on British art from 1500, and strongly supports contemporary artists. Every year the Tate hosts the Turner Prize nominees' exhibits before the winner is announced. In 1998, Tracey Emin's unmade *My Bed* was one of many pieces of art to stir up great public debate.

MILLBANK TOWER

When completed in 1963, the shiny Millbank Tower (then known as Vickers Tower) was London's tallest building. The skyscraper's 32 floors rise to 387ft (118m) above the river. Constructed from stainless steel and glass, it sits on the north bank of the Thames, about half a mile upstream from the Houses of Parliament and is now a Grade II listed building.

The tower's most famous tenant was the Labour Party, which occupied two floors from 1997 to 2001. During those four years the rent rose from £300,000 a year to £900,000. At that time the name Millbank became heavily symbolic, synonymous with political spin and tight party control of its MPs and the party across the country.

ALBERT BRIDGE

Spanning the river between Battersea and Chelsea, the Albert Bridge with its "ice-cream" colours, is London's prettiest. In 1884 the great engineer Sir Joseph Bazalgette modified the original 1873 cantilever design along the lines of a suspension bridge.

17

KENSINGTON PALACE (left)

The Royal Borough of Kensington and Chelsea boasts that Kensington Palace, at the western end of Kensington Gardens, is perhaps the finest building in the borough. William and Mary bought this Jacobean building, then known as Nottingham House, in 1689. The Kensington air was considered healthier for the King, who suffered from asthma. Sir Christopher Wren designed the Clock Court and the South Front and later, for Queen Anne, the Orangery.

This was Queen Victoria's childhood home, and the place where she was told she was to accede to the throne. In the 20th century several members of the royal family, including Diana, Princess of Wales, were granted grace-and-favour apartments here.

Successive generations of royal enthusiasts have remodelled sections of the gardens: formal gardens with fountains, summerhouses and "wilderness". George II's wife Caroline created the basic structure of the area now known as Kensington Gardens. She installed the Broad Walk, which runs north-south alongside the old gardens from the Bayswater Road to Kensington Road.

DIANA FOUNTAIN *(left)*

In July 2004 the Queen opened the Diana Memorial Fountain as a tribute to the life of Diana, Princess of Wales, who died in 1997. Even at the design stage, this oval of water, with rushing water and contemplative pools, was a controversial memorial. From the day it was opened, the project ran into problems, from leaves clogging up the channels to people slipping on the wet stone. Its accessibility, an essential element the American designer Kathryn Gustafson had expressly intended to mirror Diana's nature, has had to be restricted for public safety.

BROMPTON ORATORY *(below)*

This Roman Catholic church, known to all as the Brompton Oratory, is more properly called the Oratory of St Philip Neri. It is in flamboyant Italian baroque style, a highly decorated church that dominates its surroundings. The nave is the widest of any church in London bar Westminster Abbey. The church was restored and redecorated to mark its centenary in 1984.

HYDE PARK AND KENSINGTON GARDENS

Formerly a royal hunting ground for Henry VIII, Hyde Park became London's first public park in 1637. Some 200 years later Kensington Gardens was also gifted to the public. The two parks retain quite separate characteristics: Kensington Gardens, with its famous statue of Peter Pan and the Diana Memorial Playground, is particularly child-friendly.

In the foreground of the main picture is the Round Pond, for centuries a favourite place for young and old to sail their toy boats. In the centre, Long Water runs into the Serpentine, created by George II's wife, Caroline, in the 1730s. Horses are still exercised along the track known as Rotten Row (a corruption of the French *Route du Roi*, or King's Road), along which William III used to walk from Kensington Palace to St James's.

Concerts (right) are a regular feature of summer in Hyde Park. While the hope is always for fine weather, concert-goers usually come prepared for sun and rain.

ROYAL ALBERT HALL *(right)*

The Royal Albert Hall of Arts and Sciences was built in 1871 for just £200,000, part of the proceeds of Prince Albert's Great Exhibition of 1851 that celebrated Britain's empire and industrial power.

The huge, dramatic dome of iron and glass rises to a height of 835ft (275m), and the hall can seat 5,222 people. The Albert Hall is known worldwide as the home of the Proms summer concerts.

On the other side of Kensington Gore, Queen Victoria's elaborate Albert Memorial glints in the sunlight.

V&A MUSEUM

Museums cluster along the northern side of Cromwell Road and Exhibition Road between Queen's Gate and Brompton Road. Walking east past the Romanesque curlicues of the Natural History Museum and the plainer outline of the Science Museum, you come to the stately mix of Victorian and Edwardian styles that is the Victoria and Albert Musuem. The site is huge – 11 acres (4.45ha) in all. The V&A's collection dedicated to art and design was founded as a legacy of Prince Albert's Great Exhibition of 1851. In the intervening years keepers have sought to reflect the world's many styles and periods in applied and decorative art. The wide-ranging collection includes items as diverse as an 18th-century Norwegian drinking bowl with horse-head handles and Canova's *Three Graces*; medieval leather shoes and an early 20th-century embroidered silk tunic from Baluchistan; textiles by William Morris and Bridget Riley's Op Art silkscreen prints.

Photography started at much the same time as the museum was founded, and today the V&A holds one of the world's most important photographic collections, with more than half a million images.

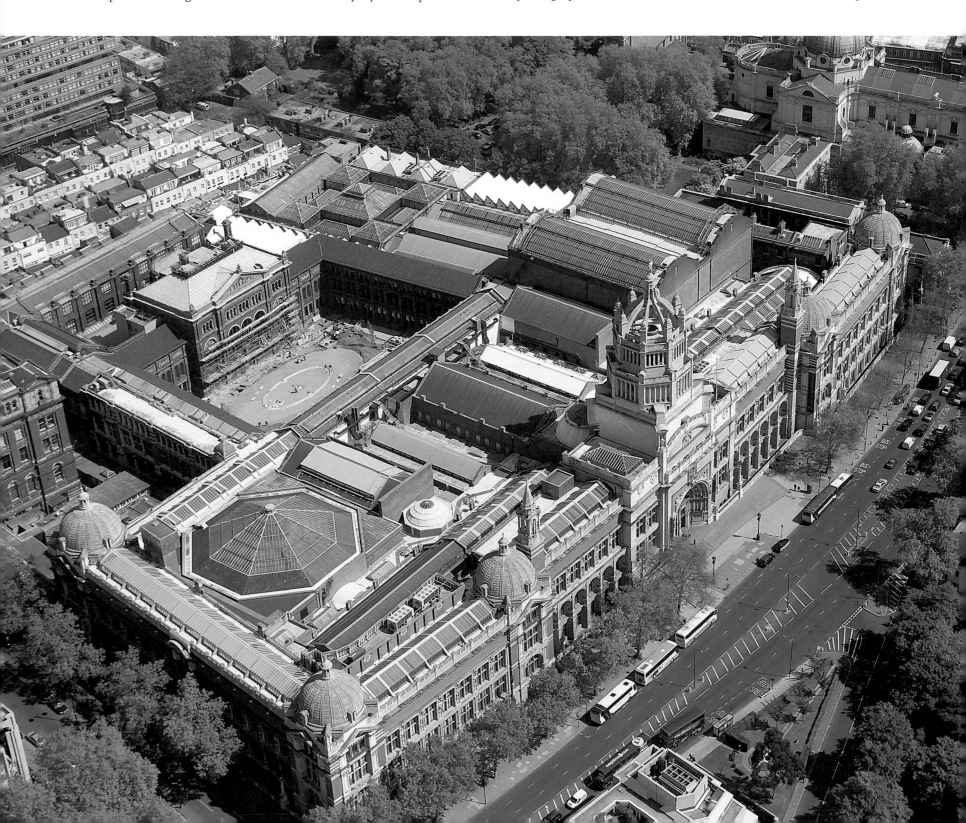

KNIGHTSBRIDGE

Household Cavalry officers based in the nearby barracks often exercise their horses early in the morning on the tracks by the Serpentine in the southern reaches of Hyde Park (above). Nearby Knightsbridge, Sloane Square, Belgravia and Chelsea are all home to the smart set in London society.

HARRODS

If you live in Knightsbridge, you may consider Harrods to be your corner shop. The enormous food hall is a feast for the eyes and the palate, and seven storeys of luxury goods await shoppers with limitless funds. This red-brick emporium is perhaps the world's most famous department store.

MARBLE ARCH (right)

John Nash designed Marble Arch as the entrance to Buckingham Palace, but it proved too narrow for grand coaches. In 1851 it was moved to become an entrance to Hyde Park, and now it sits amid the traffic at the western end of Oxford Street. Previously Tyburn Gallows stood on this site, where criminals were hanged in public from 1388 to 1793.

HYDE PARK CORNER (below)

The Wellington Arch at Hyde Park Corner has similarly lost its original purpose as an entrance to Buckingham Palace. It stands opposite Apsley House, the Duke of Wellington's London home in the years following Waterloo. At first, controversially, it was topped with a huge statue of the Duke astride a horse, but this was later replaced by *Peace in her Chariot* by Adrian Jones. The arch used to house a tiny police station.

ROYAL ACADEMY, PICCADILLY

The glorious Burlington House on Piccadilly houses the Royal Academy of Art. This is an independent fine arts institution and its members are professionally active painters, sculptors, printmakers and architects. They elect 80 Academicians to govern the Royal Academy; its collection holds one piece of work by each current and former Academician. The annual Summer Exhibition is an enormously popular gathering of contemporary art, and the Academy also hosts major art exhibitions, with more than a million visitors every year.

AMERICAN EMBASSY *(left)*

The giant eagle spreads its wings atop the American Embassy in London, which occupies the whole of the west side of Grosvenor Square. During the Second World War this area, at the heart of Mayfair, was known as Little America as General Eisenhower also had his headquarters on the square. Today the gardens retain a strongly American presence, with memorials to Eisenhower, Roosevelt and those who lost their lives in the terrorist attacks on the US on September 11, 2001.

ST JAMES'S

The palace of St James and its neighbour, Clarence House, look across the Mall to the intimate charms of St James's Park. The park is quite different in character from its neighbour, Green Park. Charles II commissioned a Frenchman to transform Henry VIII's deer park into a garden, complete with an aviary (hence Birdcage Walk, the road that borders the southern side of the park).

Foreign ambassadors are accredited to the Court of St James as this is still officially regarded as the headquarters of the royal court, though the royal family lives in Buckingham Palace. Clarence House was the home of the Queen Mother until her death in 2002, and is now the London home of the Prince of Wales.

REGENT STREET

Regent Street sweeps from Langham Place to the north, across Oxford Street and then down between Soho and Mayfair in an elegant and orderly curve. Around Piccadilly Circus and then along the last section of Regent Street, you finally arrive at Pall Mall, just in front of Carlton Terrace. This was where the Prince Regent had a house in the 1820s. When he asked John Nash to create a processional route from Carlton House to Regent's Park, Nash designed a broad thoroughfare with fashionable shops, which held disreputable Soho at bay.

Today shops are very much at the heart of Regent Street. Highly respected old favourites such as Liberty, Burberry, Austin Reed and Hamley's, London's largest toyshop, vie for the passing shoppers with many of the more recent chainstores. The newcomers have had to fit in, however, and the character of the street remains largely unchanged.

27

PICCADILLY CIRCUS
(left and right)
Piccadilly Circus' famous giant neon signs glitter, night and day. This is perhaps London's most visited spot, a meeting place and junction of five major roads. Haymarket and Shaftesbury Avenue's theatres meet the shops of Regent Street and Piccadilly, while in the back streets, pubs and nightclubs compete with restaurants and cinemas for customers. Tourists meet by the statue of Eros *(right)* before heading for Carnaby Street, Soho and Leicester Square nearby.

And the name Piccadilly? A fashionable lace collar in the 17th century, known as a *picadil*, was the stock-in-trade of a successful dressmaker who bought a house nearby.

TRAFALGAR SQUARE

The open space and dramatic backdrop of Trafalgar Square has long been a focal point for political rallies, from the Chartists in 1848 to the anti-apartheid protests outside South Africa House throughout the 1960s, 70s and 80s. Every Christmas, Norway sends a huge tree to stand here in thanks for Britain's support in the Second World War.

The northern side of Trafalgar Square is entirely taken up by the National Gallery, which houses one of the world's finest collections of European paintings.

NELSON'S COLUMN

John Nash designed Trafalgar Square as a tribute to Horatio Nelson, after the admiral's victory over the combined French and Spanish fleets at the Battle of Trafalgar in 1805. The square's focal point is a 184ft (56m) tall granite column. The 14 stonemasons who worked on the column celebrated its completion by dining on the flat top before installing Nelson's 18ft (5.5m) statue.

Symbolic bronze castings at the top of the column were cast from British cannon, while the bronze reliefs at the foot of the column, showing Nelson's four major victories, were made from captured French and Spanish guns. Four giant bronze lions by Landseer gaze outward from the corners of the pedestal.

CENTRE POINT

At the heart of the West End stands Centre Point, described by Jonathan Glancey in the Guardian as "that 385ft beehive hairdo rising in tiers of pristine white concrete from the cramped road junction at St Giles Circus at the east end of London's Oxford Street". Thirty-five floors were built with huge prefabricated H-shaped units of pre-cast concrete. After completion in 1964 the block stood empty for many years, a source of much controversy.

OXFORD STREET *(right)*

What some people today consider one and a half miles of retail heaven, was once part of the Roman road from Hampshire to Colchester. It was only in the latter part of the 18th century that building began on the surrounding fields here. In the 1870s DH Evans and John Lewis set up shop on Oxford Street, to be followed 40 years later by Harry Gordon Selfridge. Oxford Street now claims one of the world's highest concentrations of large shops, with about 200m shoppers and an annual turnover of £6bn. Four busy underground stations, Marble Arch, Bond Street, Oxford Circus and Tottenham Court Road serve Oxford Street, as well as 39 bus routes. Private cars are banned but the street is regularly at a standstill, with some 250 buses and 750 taxis an hour.

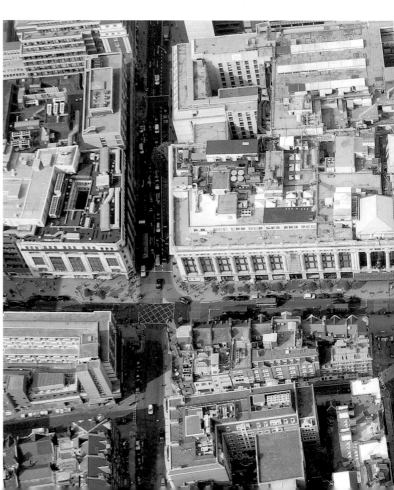

LEICESTER SQUARE *(above)*

The square now dominated by cinema multiplexes and the Swiss
Centre (where the cowherd clock chimes every hour) was once an
elegant residential address. Isaac Newton, an early resident, is
commemorated with a bust in the south-west corner of the
square's gardens. Joshua Reynolds painted portraits of society's
elite in his elegant studio at 46 Leicester Square. The artist
William Hogarth's house later became the Hotel de la Sablionère,
one of the area's first public restaurants.

By the 1980s Leicester Square had become rather seedy, but in
1993 Westminster council cleaned it up. The reinvigorated square
now offers pavement cafes and is always busy. Every day a crowd
gathers at the Half-Price Ticket Booth to buy low-cost tickets for
theatre performances the same day. A statue of Charlie Chaplin
stands here, a fitting tribute in a square that regularly sees the UK
premieres of major films.

SAVOY PLACE *(above)*

Just west of Waterloo Bridge, set between the River Thames and the Strand, stands Shell Mex House with its central clock tower, and the Savoy Hotel. Richard D'Oyly Carte capitalised on the success of his Savoy Theatre by building a luxurious hotel next door. The resulting Art Deco gem was run by César Ritz, with Auguste Escoffier as the master chef.

CHARING CROSS

A cross in front of Charing Cross Station marks the spot where the funeral procession of Edward the Confessor's beloved wife Eleanor rested on the way to Westminster in 1290. Charing Cross is one of the great Victorian railway stations, opened in 1864 to bring trains from Kent into the very centre of London. Behind it, the spire of St Martin-in-the-Fields church on Trafalgar Square just catches the sun.

SOMERSET HOUSE

From late November to January the peaceful Fountain Court at
Somerset House becomes a temporary ice rink. This inspired move,
originally to mark the Millennium in 2000, has in a short time
become a treasured highlight of London's winter scene. The classical
facades of the surrounding 18th-century masterpiece are home to
several remarkable art galleries including the Courtauld and Gilbert
collections, and works from the Hermitage Museum in St Petersburg.

The whole of Somerset House was designed as a series of town-
houses, each with six storeys including two below ground and one in
the roof. By concealing such a significant part of the accommodation,
the architect Sir William Chambers succeeded in reconciling the
practicalities of housing several prestigious learned societies and
government departments with the demand for an impressive
building that would be "an object of national splendour".

THEATRELAND AND COVENT GARDEN
(above and right)

With the Strand to the south and Shaftesbury Avenue
to the north, this is the heart of London's theatreland.
Some theatres, like the Prince of Wales on Coventry Street
(right) have undergone renovations every bit as dramatic
as anything on their stage. Inevitably the area is also rich
in restaurants of all types.

Just behind the Royal Opera House is Covent Garden
(above), London's first attempt at town planning. Inigo Jones'
16th-century piazza with arcaded houses on two sides was
hugely influenced by the public squares and classical
architecture he had seen in Italy. The straight streets with
which he surrounded the piazza were quite different from
London's traditionally haphazard arrangements.

By the late 19th century the name Covent Garden had
become synonymous with its fruit and vegetable market.
Traffic congestion forced the market to move out to Nine
Elms in 1973. The piazza's old market buildings now house
many boutiques, craft stalls, pavement cafes and restaurants.

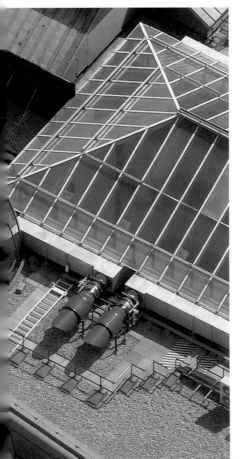

ROYAL OPERA HOUSE (above)

Popularly referred to by opera enthusiasts as Covent Garden and by its employees as the House, the Royal Opera House continues a tradition of opera here since 1732. This is the third theatre to occupy the site. After the Second World War the public gradually accepted that the arts should be subsidised and the Royal Opera House became the permanent home of the opera and ballet companies. Recent refurbishment of the building has been radical and the emphasis has been on making the House accessible to the wider community, not just opera and ballet lovers. During the day you can view the refurbished Floral Hall (the curved roof to the left of the grand entrance) and make your way to the Amphitheatre Bar for views of the costume-making department and out over Covent Garden.

SEVEN DIALS (right)

Seven streets come together at Seven Dials, named after the sundials on the pillar at the junction. The cobbled streets run between Shaftesbury Avenue and Covent Garden. Shops selling up-to-the-minute fashions and streetwear mix with vintage boutiques, while exclusive restaurants such as the Ivy and Carluccio's delicatessen are complemented by wholefoods and complementary therapies in Neal's Yard.

ALDWYCH

At the southern end of Kingsway, Bush House, the home of the BBC World Service, occupies the central tranche of the Aldwych crescent. The motto above the portico reads "Friendship Between English-speaking Peoples"; in fact, this section of the BBC broadcasts in 43 languages. The World Service moved here from Portland Place in 1941 after Broadcasting House was damaged in an air raid. At the far left of the picture above is Marconi House. Guglielmo Marconi and his associates made the first commercial broadcast from the seventh floor in May 1922. Sandwiched between Marconi House and Bush House is India House. In 1929, four Bengali artists travelled to Europe to learn techniques for painting on plaster. On their return to London they painted murals throughout India House, and worked together for 10 months to convey India's history in the spectacular central dome.

ST MARY LE STRAND

To the south of Aldwych, on its own island in the middle of the Strand, stands the elegant little church of St Mary le Strand. It is highly decorated, with carved stone facings both inside and out. The windows are placed high in the walls to keep out the noise that was already a feature of the Strand in the 18th century. James Gibbs' original design included a column to mark Queen Anne's active support for the building of 50 new churches to serve London's growing population. However, after the Jacobite rebellion, the column was abandoned and Gibbs designed a delicate spire to house the church bell.

Travelling down Kingsway towards the Aldwych, the buildings on the left are part of the London School of Economics and Politics (LSE). Thirteen Nobel prizewinners, including George Bernard Shaw, have been alumni of the LSE.

ST CLEMENT DANES (above)

Dedicated to the Royal Air Force, St Clement Dane's sits
surrounded by trees at the eastern end of the Strand. It was
rebuilt by William the Conqueror and later by Sir Christopher
Wren. This is the church that inspired the nursery rhyme
Oranges and Lemons: when a boat arrived at the nearby wharf on
the Thames with a cargo of citrus fruit, it is said that the bells
were rung. St Clement Dane's was largely destroyed by bombs
during the Blitz. The interior was completely rebuilt in 1958.

Australia House, at the top of this picture, completes the
Aldwych crescent. In 1912 the appalling slums, so vividly
described by Charles Dickens, were demolished to make way
for Kingsway and Aldwych. The Australian government bought
the plot, to the east of what is now Bush House, for £1m. This
limestone building, opened in 1918, is Australia's oldest
diplomatic mission abroad.

In the foreground of the picture is the imposing front
elevation of the Royal Courts of Justice.

ROYAL COURTS OF JUSTICE *(below)*

Where the Strand becomes Fleet Street, this dramatic Victorian Gothic building is set back from the road. It has some 1,000 rooms, over three miles of corridors and 88 courtrooms. Also known as the Law Courts, the Royal Courts of Justice are the UK's main civil courts. The High Court here takes the most important divorce, libel and civil liability cases and appeals.

On the second Saturday in November, the new Lord Mayor of the City of London continues a 400-year tradition by coming to the Royal Courts of Justice to swear allegiance to the Queen. A flamboyant parade marks the occasion, with over 6,000 people, bands and performers and about 140 floats. The Lord Mayor travels in a gilded horse-drawn coach with members of the Company of Pikemen and Musketeers forming a bodyguard.

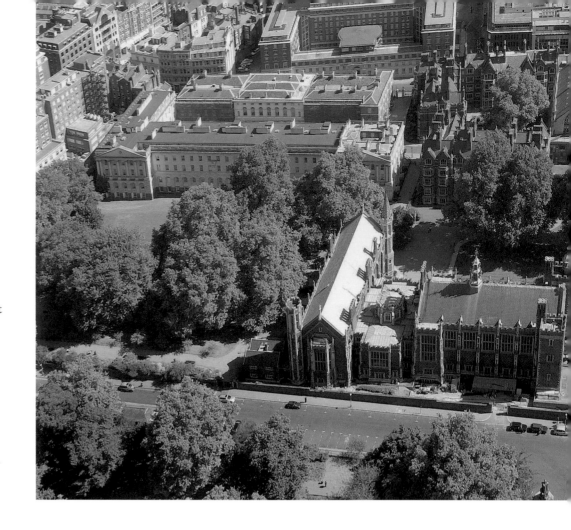

LINCOLN'S INN CHAPEL *(left)*

The largest square in London, Lincoln's Inn Fields is a green oasis to the south of Holborn. Lincoln's Inn is one of the four Inns of Court – the others are Gray's Inn, Middle Temple and Inner Temple. Tradition dictates that barristers must belong to one of the Inns, pass examinations and dine there 24 times before gaining their qualification.

The Gothic chapel was built in the early 17th century, and until 1839 only men could be buried here. Most of the pews are original, made in 1623 at a cost of £220. The bell tolls 60 times each night at 9pm. Desperate mothers left their babies here, knowing that Lincoln's Inn would ensure their wellbeing. These foundlings were usually given the surname Lincoln.

TEMPLE GARDENS

Three acres of well-tended gardens make this one of London's loveliest spaces. It is quite a well-kept secret: few people know that it is open to the public on weekday afternoons. Flowerbeds are planted with alternate white and red roses, to mark the Wars of the Roses, England's dynastic struggles between 1453 and 1485.

All round the gardens are prestigious chambers for barristers: to the left, Middle Temple Lane, to the right, King's Bench Walk.

BRITISH MUSEUM

At the heart of Bloomsbury, the British Museum first opened in 1759. It was free and open to "all studious and curious Persons" and has remained open continuously since then, with the exception of the two world wars. Today some five million people visit the museum every year. The Elgin Marbles from the Parthenon in Athens are among the museum's most controversial treasures.

The wide-ranging collection of art and artefacts began as a bequest of 71,000 objects from Sir Hans Sloane, a naturalist and physician. In the 1850s the quadrangular building was built to house the rapidly growing museum, together with the domed Reading Room for the British Library.

The natural history collection moved to South Kensington in the 1880s, and in 1998 the British Library moved to St Pancras. The spectacular glass roof over the Great Court was completed in 2000 when the Reading Room was re-opened to the public.

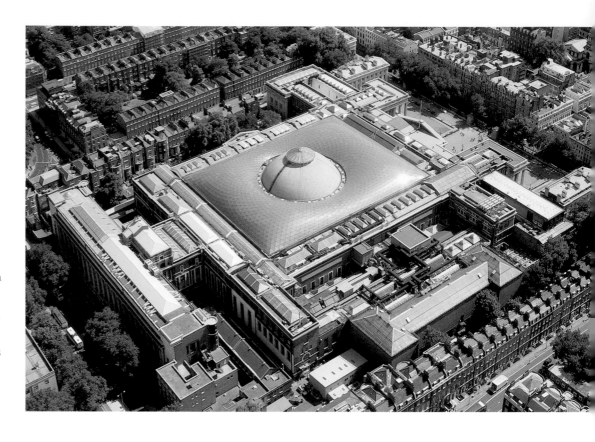

PRUDENTIAL BUILDING (above)

The huge red-brick Prudential building on High Holborn stands on the old site of Furnival's Inn, where Charles Dickens started writing *The Pickwick Papers*. The brief for the architect, Alfred Waterhouse, in 1879 was to design a head office for the Prudential insurance company that was "good, but not apparently costly". By 1906 it was a modern marvel, with central heating, electric clocks and pneumatic tubes to speed documents around the building. At the time the company proudly featured a Lady Clerks department, employing women between 18-25 who had their own entrance, offices, library, dining room and roof terrace. The "Pru" also embraced new technology, acquiring a typewriter and 24 "arithmometer" calculating machines in 1871. The renovated building is no longer the company's main office.

VICTORIA HOUSE, BLOOMSBURY SQUARE (left)

This neo-classical building is Victoria House, commissioned in the 1930s as the London headquarters of the Liverpool Victoria Friendly Society (now relocated to Bournemouth). The refurbished building retains many of its glorious Art Deco features.

BLOOMSBURY *(above)*

In the early 20th century this district, centred around Bloomsbury Square, was synonymous with the Bloomsbury Group of writers and artists. The most famous member of the group, the writer Virginia Woolf, lived in a succession of five houses in Bloomsbury, only two of which remain standing today.

Bloomsbury Square was built in 1661, the first in this previously rural area. Over the next 200 years several other grand squares were laid out, including Russell Square and Bedford Square, and while the area became a popular place to live, it was never really seen as a fashionable district. Many of the Georgian buildings here belong to the University of London which, together with the British Museum, still dominates Bloomsbury today.

FITZROVIA *(right)*

To the west of Bloomsbury, on the other side of Tottenham Court Road, lies Fitzrovia, much of which was designed by Robert Adam. This quiet, slightly shabby area contrasts with the bustle of Tottenham Court Road. The Fitzroy Tavern in Charlotte Street was a favourite haunt of George Orwell, Dylan Thomas and their circle of writers and friends between the two world wars.

TELECOM TOWER

It seems incredible that such a conspicuous landmark as this 620ft (189m) tower on Cleveland Street should ever have been classed an official secret – no Ordnance Survey maps showed it until the middle of the 1990s, and strictly speaking it was an offence under the Official Secrets Act to take or possess photographs of the tower.

The Grade II listed tower was the first to be built specifically for the transmission of high-frequency radio waves, and still transmits broadcast, internet and telephone information. For 16 years this was London's tallest building. When it opened in 1965 it was known as the Post Office Tower, and 1.5m people came to see it during that first year. It was subsequently renamed the BT Tower or Telecom Tower.

Its circular shape reduces wind resistance, and was intended to survive the blast wave from a nuclear bomb. The top floors were designed as observation galleries, but were closed to the public after a bomb exploded in 1971. The slowly revolving restaurant closed nine years later, although it is occasionally hired for corporate entertaining.

EUSTON *(above)*

Little remains today of the station that was built here in the 1830s as the terminus for the London and Birmingham Railway. At first there were just two platforms – one for arrivals, the other for departures. The station was expanded piecemeal to cater for the increase in rail traffic to Scotland and northern England. In the 1960s just two Portland Stone lodges and a war memorial at the Euston Road entrance survived the radical redesign of Euston station, at the same time as the West Coast main line was electrified.

The modern station has 20 platforms, and about 70 trains come in and out of it every day. With a busy underground station as well, some 51 million people pass through Euston annually.

BRITISH LIBRARY *(right)*

When the purpose-built British Library was opened by the Queen in June 1998, it brought together several significant national collections, including the library of the British Museum. That library was founded on George II's gift of the Old Royal Library in 1757.

The British Library receives a copy of every publication issued in the UK and Ireland. The huge collection grows by 3 million items every year, ranging from books, newspapers and maps to music, DVDs and stamps. In 2005 these were housed on more than 390 miles (625km) of shelving – and 7.5 miles (12km) is added every year.

Among the British Library's treasures is the Magna Carta, the charter signed by King John in 1215 that first restricted the absolute power of the monarch, as well as the fabulously illuminated Anglo-Saxon Lindisfarne Gospels, and the Gutenberg Bible, Europe's first real book printed from moveable type.

KING'S CROSS AND ST PANCRAS *(above)*

To the east of the British Library stand two completely contrasting stations, St Pancras and King's Cross. St Pancras is generally recognised by the red brick High Gothic frontage: this is not the station, but St Pancras Chambers, offices that started life in 1874 as the Midland Grand Hotel. Tucked behind, St Pancras station opened two years later, its enormous roof the largest in the world at that time. Trains come in to the station at first-floor level.

The earthworks seen to the north are the London end of the final part of the high-speed Channel Tunnel Rail Link. Work is due to be completed in 2007, when St Pancras International will become the London terminus for all Eurostar trains.

The cross that gave King's Cross its name was raised in 1836, in memory of George IV. A smallpox hospital used to stand here. When the original station was built in the 1850s, it included stabling for 300 horses, an essential in those pre-motor car days. The station design was functional rather than elaborate, its main feature the two curved roofs of the train sheds. In the steam era this was a trainspotter's paradise, as the *Flying Scotsman* regularly set off from King's Cross to Edinburgh.

REGENT'S PARK AND MARYLEBONE ROAD *(below)*

The lush greenery of Regent's Park offsets the elegant buildings of Regent's College on the other side of the boating lake. Regent's Canal (right) skirts the northern edge of the park before winding up through Camden.

Like an alien spaceship, the dome of the London Planetarium sits on Marylebone Road. Next door is the ever-popular waxworks exhibition, Madame Tussaud's. On nearby Baker Street in 1815, Madame Tussaud first displayed the wax death masks she had made of famous victims of the guillotine during the French Revolution. Traditional techniques are still used, although today whole body wax models are generally made while the celebrities are still alive.

Baker Street runs south from Regent's Park. When Conan Doyle based his fictional detective at 221B, this address did not exist. In the 1930s Baker Street was extended north, and 221 became the offices of the Abbey building society. Every month the office responds to dozens of letters that still arrive, addressed to Sherlock Holmes.

The bold white buildings of the University of Westminster's Marylebone campus, and its tower block student accommodation, dominate the southern side of Marylebone Road.

BROADCASTING HOUSE, PORTLAND PLACE *(below)*

The BBC's headquarters on Langham Place, at the southern end of Portland Place, were purpose-built for the radio services in 1932. Three of the 12 floors of this art deco building are underground. It has a ship-like appearance, but from the seventh floor up it is not symmetrical: the original design was adapted when neighbours protested that it was depriving them of daylight.

PORTLAND PLACE *(above)*

Much of Portland Place was designed by Robert and James Adams in the late 18th century. These Scottish brothers were deeply inspired by styles fashionable in Italy at the time, neo-classical, baroque and rococo. The challenge was to honour the gentleman's agreement between the Duke of Portland and Lord Foley, that no buildings would obscure Foley's view of Regent's Park from the southern end of the street. The resulting broad avenue makes its stately way, curving round the colonnaded terraces of Park Crescent before reaching Regent's Park.

Parallel to Portland Place runs Harley Street to the west (left in this picture). For more than 150 years Harley Street has been the ultimate address for medical practitioners and today about 1,500 doctors and dentists pursue their private practice here.

ST JOHN'S WOOD (left) AND LORD'S CRICKET GROUND (above)

April sees the start of the cricketing season in England. The world-famous wicket at Lord's, the cricket ground of the Marylebone Cricket Club (better known as the MCC), is the scene every year of memorable cricket matches, from village and club finals to Middlesex home games, Test matches and one-day internationals. In the 1820s, the wicket was "prepared" by grazing sheep – today a team of professionals tend the immaculate grass to a standard by which all other grounds are measured. The MCC is the guardian of the laws and spirit of cricket.

The Regent's Canal branch of the Grand Union Canal is visible as it winds through the exclusive residential area of St John's Wood, to the west of Regent's Park.

REGENT'S PARK MOSQUE

By the outbreak of the Second World War the British Empire had more Muslim inhabitants than Christian. In recognition of the many thousands of Muslim soldiers who died in defence of the Empire, Winston Churchill's government gifted 2.3 acres (0.93ha) near Hanover Gate in Regent's Park to the Muslim community. The mosque and Islamic Cultural Centre were completed in 1977.

The City

AT THE HEART of the capital of the United Kingdom stands the City of London. Just 7,000 people live in this small area, but every day 300,000 commuters come in to work in one of the world's leading international financial centres. Historic privileges ensure that the City remains distinct from the rest of London. The Corporation of London runs the City, its police force and schools and is presided over by a Lord Mayor, aldermen and councillors who are elected by residents and businesspeople.

The City has seen more than its fair share of disaster, from the Plague and Great Fire of London in two successive years (1665-1666) to the months of the Blitz during the Second World War. After each tragedy the City has risen like a phoenix and gained strength in its renewal.

Bank *above*, and looking west, the Thames with Tower Bridge in the foreground

THE SQUARE MILE

The City is also known as the Square Mile, although in fact it covers a slightly larger area. This is the historic heart of London: traces of the Roman city walls remain, and its boundaries now are more or less those that were in place during the Middle Ages.

The Square Mile stretches from Victoria Embankment at its southern edge to Middle Temple in the west, north to Chancery Lane, the Barbican and east to Liverpool Street and Aldgate.

The City has an importance quite disproportionate to its size. It is an economic powerhouse, with more than 500 financial institutions. People say there are more Japanese and American banks here than in Tokyo or New York. The City is in effect an enclave, with its own mayor, who is elected annually by the business community. The Lord Mayor of London becomes head of the Corporation of London, the City's governing body and travels widely as an advocate for the City's business community. Only one woman has been elected to this post since the Middle Ages.

In the past 50 years the skyline has been dramatically altered by bold architectural statements, such as the Swiss Re building (known as the Gherkin) and Tower 42 (still widely known as the NatWest tower), seen here at the centre of the photograph (above).

TOWER BRIDGE

An unusual view (*left*) of one of London's greatest landmarks. The Corporation of London commissioned this key crossing point in the late 1880s to link the City and East London to London's suburbs to the south-east. The original mechanism which raised the central bascules was steam-driven, but today it is electrically-powered.

On a good day you may see the central sections of Tower Bridge lift three or four times to allow cruise ships, naval vessels and tall ships to pass between the upper and lower parts of the Pool of London.

At its peak, Tower Bridge was raised about 6,000 times a year; it still opens about 600 times annually and spectators are often surprised to see the bascules rise in less than two minutes.

THAMES AT TOWER BRIDGE

The River Thames is surely one of the great sights of London as it weaves eastwards through the City on its way to the sea. It was not always a thing of joy: for centuries the Thames acted as a conduit for all London's human and industrial waste. In the 14th century Edward III was so outraged after travelling by boat on the river that he complained to the city councillors about "the fumes and other abominable stenches arising therefrom". The modern river is clean enough to attract salmon that swim upstream to spawn.

On the northern bank *(below)* rises the modern outline of the Tower hotel, with views over Tower Bridge to the front and St Katharine Docks behind. The outer reaches of the Tower of London are just visible to the west of the bridge.

ST KATHARINE DOCKS *(above and right)*

The redevelopment of St Katharine Docks in the 1970s transformed the fortunes of the area, giving rise to Docklands' reputation in the late 20th century as a fashionable place for London's young urban professionals to live and work.

The history of this part of London is richer than the current buildings suggest. At the start of the 19th century the longstanding community here had its own church, school and court. This was all swept away for a huge enclosed dock with berths for 120 ships, and giant warehouses. But by the 1930s ships were too large to berth here and St Katharine's role diminished to specialised storage. After much of the dock and surrounding warehousing was damaged during air raids in the Second World War, the complex fell into disuse.

The buildings around the dock now house the London Futures and Options Exchange, restaurants, offices and shops. At their heart is a stunning yacht marina.

TOWER HILL

Two thousand years of history can be seen in the photograph above. In the early years of the first millennium, the Roman emperor Claudius erected a fortress on Tower Hill to defend his new acquisition, *Londinium*. Ten centuries later the keep of William the Conqueror's stronghold incorporated a section of the Roman wall. The Tower of London continued to evolve as a palace and a fortress, witnessing many dramatic events in Britain's turbulent history. Today it functions principally as a historical museum, housing treasures including the Crown Jewels, and is among Britain's most popular tourist attractions. Sited immediately opposite is one of the architectural highlights of 21st-century London – City Hall, designed by the architect Norman Foster and opened in 2002.

Moving east, Tower Bridge stands witness to the ingenuity and engineering prowess of the Victorian era. Meanwhile, on the other side of the approach road to Tower Bridge, the ultra-modern complex of the St Katharine Docks reflects commercial and residential aspirations at the end of the 20th century.

THE TOWER OF LONDON

The deep moat that used to separate the inhabitants and prisoners of the Tower of London was drained by Queen Victoria and now cuts a broad green swathe around the battlements. The Tower's prisoners arrived by boat at the Traitor's Gate, and many waited years before being beheaded on Tower Green, or hanged in public on Tower Hill. One prisoner who left intact and returned as Queen was Elizabeth I. The remains of those less fortunate were buried here in the chapel of St Peter ad Vincula (St Peter in chains).

The Tower of London is a complex of 13 towers and other houses, with the White Tower (*below*), built of stone specially imported from France by William the Conqueror, at its heart. It was however more than a prison: at various times it has housed a royal palace, an arsenal, the Royal Mint and even a zoo.

UNDERWRITING CENTRE AND POOL OF LONDON

Insurance is a vital activity in the City of London. The London Underwriting Centre (right) opened in 1993 as a marketplace for the world's leading insurance companies. At one time, most of the ships that passed through the London Docks would have been insured by City institutions. The stretch of the Thames known as the Pool of London (between London Bridge and Tower Bridge) was vital to the nation's trading success. Hay's Wharf, built in the 1850s, was the first to offer cold storage for perishable foodstuffs while Butler's Wharf specialised in tea, coffee and spices. Tower Bridge, with its central opening span allowed tall ships to pass through into the Upper Pool. But by the turn of the century vessels were becoming ever larger until, by the 1960s, Tilbury docks downriver in Essex had become London's main trading port.

LONDON BRIDGE *(above)*

When the Saxons pulled down London Bridge in 1014 to recapture London from the Danes, they inspired the famous nursery rhyme *London Bridge is falling down*. The bridge rebuilt, this remained the only place to cross the Thames in London for 700 years. In the Middle Ages traitors' heads were displayed on the Southwark end as a warning to all. In 1973 the picturesque old bridge was shipped to Arizona, and replaced with the one you see today.

MONUMENT *(right)*

Many Londoners probably have no idea what the world's highest freestanding stone column commemorates. It is 202ft (61.5m) tall and you can climb its 311 steps to the observation platform for a glorious view of the City of London. From here it is 202ft to the spot in Pudding Lane where the Great Fire of London began in 1666 – the event that the architect Sir Christopher Wren honoured with the Monument.

LIVERPOOL STREET STATION

This is the terminus for trains to the north-east of London, the east coast of England and Stansted Airport. Much has changed since the grimy days of steam trains: redevelopment in the 1980s ensured the station is relatively light and airy while retaining elements of its 19th-century grandeur. Liverpool Street is the side street visible here. The station's main entrance lies on the broad sweep of Bishopsgate.

BROAD STREET *(right)*

The bold 1980s redevelopment of the area around Liverpool Street station included a huge commercial complex now known as Broadgate. The Broadgate Arena, seen here, was built on the site of the old Broad Street station. In the summer this is a favoured spot for office workers to pause and listen to the lunchtime concerts, while from November to April the central circle becomes a very popular ice rink.

FINSBURY CIRCUS *(left)*

Between the non-stop traffic of Moorgate and the trains of Liverpool Street lies an ellipse of tranquillity, Finsbury Circus. Its terraces of grand offices house major companies such as BP and echo the curves of the garden. At the heart of the public gardens are the beautifully kept lawns of the City of London Bowls Club.

CITY OF LONDON FESTIVAL

As part of the City of London Festival, office workers and passers-by can enjoy free lunchtime concerts in Finsbury Circus Gardens from the end of June to the middle of July every year. In addition to ticketed events with notable music and dance stars, the festival offers more than 60 free outdoor events, ranging from street theatre, world music and dance to brass bands and jazz concerts.

SWISS RE BUILDING

The organic shape of the Swiss Re building at 30 St Mary Axe has been variously described as a pine cone, a poplar and a cigar, but the most popular epithet remains "the Gherkin". Designed by Norman Foster, it won the RIBA Stirling prize as the most innovative and well-designed British building completed in 2004. With 40 floors rising to 590ft (180m), it stands on the site of the Baltic Exchange which was destroyed by an IRA bomb in 1992.

The continuous elegant curve of this stunning building broke with the orthodoxy of skyscrapers the world over and soon became very popular with most people living and working nearby. The shape is designed to be aerodynamically efficient, with no dramatic downdraughts buffeting passers-by, and is energy-efficient with minimal need for air-conditioning and windows that can be opened by the office workers inside. The full-time job of cleaning the windows can only be undertaken safely when the wind speed is less than 21mph.

TOWER 42 *(below)*

The footprint of Tower 42, formerly known as the NatWest Tower, reflected the three V-shapes of the logo of National Westminster Bank, which commissioned the building on Old Broad Street. It held the title of London's tallest building from its opening in 1980 until the completion of Canary Wharf 10 years later.

The NatWest Tower was the City's first skyscraper. At the time it was a controversial structure, with cantilevered floors extending from a huge concrete core. This core made it very strong, but took up a huge amount of space.

The bank moved out after the tower was severely damaged by an IRA bomb in 1993. The building was restored as a general office building, with a number of companies coming in as tenants. Today it remains one of the structures that dominate London's skyline, but inspires little affection in Londoners.

SMITHFIELD (left)

The fascinating names of the tiny streets around Smithfield meat market, such as Giltspur Street and Hosier Lane, echo its strong medieval links. London's oldest inhabited house at 41-42 Cloth Fair survived the Great Fire of London in 1666. The cloth fair that gave the street its name was an annual event until 1855 in the grounds of St Bartholomew-the-Great. You still approach this remarkable Norman church through a 13th-century half-timbered archway on Little Britain.

The "smooth field" here witnessed everything from jousting to mass burnings of heretics. The wholesale meat market based at Smithfield continues a tradition that has lasted more than 800 years. Originally held in the open air, the market is now housed in the great halls you see today, opened in 1868.

The residents and workers here are fiercely proud of its teaching hospital, Barts, and resisted government efforts to close it in the early 1990s. Founded in 1123 on West Smithfield to treat the sick poor, it is now a specialist cancer and cardiac hospital.

THE BARBICAN

The 16th-century church of St Giles, Cripplegate nestles somewhat incongruously in the concrete maze of the Barbican. This was the only building in the area to survive the bombs of the Second World War. Today it serves as parish church to the 4,000 or so residents of the Barbican's 21 apartment blocks. These residents account for five-sixths of all those who live in the City of London. The angular lines of the Barbican complex were seen as a strong modern statement. While the gaunt profile of the tower blocks, with their raised walkways and bewildering layout, was widely criticised from the outset, the dynamic arts centre at the heart of the Barbican has become popular with the public since it opened in 1982. Some of the performance halls – a concert hall, two theatres and a cinema – are underground.

LLOYDS BUILDING

Richard Rogers' bold headquarters building for the insurers Lloyds of London refined some of his groundbreaking ideas from the Pompidou Centre in Paris. All the mechanical parts needing frequent maintenance, such as lifts and the 49 miles of ducts and pipes, sit on the outside of the structure and the enormous central atrium reaches up through 14 floors. The building's steel frame is clearly visible and clad with a glass curtain wall. The whole building glows blue at night.

THE GUILDHALL *(below)*

The Guildhall, begun in 1411, survived the Great Fire of London in 1666 and remains the administrative office of the City of London today. Every year the Prime Minister speaks at the Lord Mayor's inaugural banquet in the imposing Great Hall.

NO 1 POULTRY

Modern London is finding novel ways to combine commercial needs with the simple human need for greenery and fresh air. Where space is at a premium, developers and designers are increasingly looking skywards and using intensive green roofs with a deep growing medium that supports trees and bushes.

The resulting spaces can be simply stunning when viewed from the air. Diners at Terence Conran's rooftop restaurant le Coq d'Argent, at No 1 Poultry, enjoy views over City landmarks such as St Paul's Cathedral. The two dramatic roof gardens designed by Arabella Lennox-Boyd sit high above the bustle of the nine streets that meet at the Bank of England. This remarkable oasis tops a wedge-shaped post-modern building with shops and offices opposite Mansion House.

BANK

The single word "Bank" speaks volumes to Londoners.
This is in effect the heart of the City, a place where
business and finance come together. The key buildings
of the Mansion House (the Lord Mayor's official
residence), the Royal Exchange (the former home of
the London Stock Exchange) and the Bank of England
dominate the centre of this busy junction.

Heading south towards the river, Southwark Bridge
and the white squareness of Cannon Street Station is
just at the left edge of the photograph above. The bold
outline of Tower 42 looks out across Threadneedle
Street to the Lloyds Building on Lime Street.

The area takes its name from the Bank of England,
"the Old Lady of Threadneedle Street". Much of the
façade still survives from Sir John Soane's design of
1788, including the familiar colonnades on the north-
west corner, which he based on the Temple of Vesta
in Tivoli, Italy. Quaintly, the offices inside are known
as "parlours".

ROYAL EXCHANGE

At first glance the neo-classical Royal Exchange looks more like a temple. Until 1972 it housed the London Stock Exchange, which was established in 1565 by Sir Thomas Gresham as a "comely bourse for merchants to assemble on". Subsequent buildings burned down in 1666 and 1838.

From the late 18th century to 1928 the Royal Exchange was the home of Lloyds, the London insurance market.

With Threadneedle Steet and Cornhill flanking the Royal Exchange, its portico leads to a mall with a clutch of designer shops.

ST PAUL'S CATHEDRAL

When work started on Sir Christopher Wren's masterpiece, the architect was 44 years old. Thirty-five years later, in 1711 he saw the cathedral completed.

Based on the shape of a traditional Latin cross, St Paul's draws on the many building styles that Wren had admired in Europe. He was determined that the cathedral should have a dramatic focus, and designed the 360ft (110m) dome to draw the eye from afar and raise the spirit of all who entered. Wren visited every year until his death at the age of 90, to sit beneath the great dome. He is buried in St Paul's crypt alongside many of Britain's great and famous.

Every day Great Paul (at 17 tonnes England's largest bell) tolls at one o'clock. The bell is housed in one of St Paul's twin baroque towers.

THE STREETS OF LONDON

Several streets around St Paul's Cathedral reflect its religious mission: Amen Corner, Ave Maria Lane, Paternoster Row, Creed Lane and Godliman Street. Others echo the area's historic association with crime and punishment: Old Bailey, Newgate Street (site of London's main prison in the early 19th century) and Ludgate Hill, site of a medieval debtors' prison.

BLACKFRIARS BRIDGE

Blackfriars Bridge is named after the monks who had lived on the northern side of the river since 1274. The original, London's third bridge, opened in 1769. Exactly 100 years later two bridges, one for trains and one for the road, replaced it. Each column of the road bridge's polished red granite supports a small bay where people can stand and watch the river traffic. Ornate cast-iron balustrades enhance the Venetian-Gothic style.

OLD BAILEY
(above and left)

As you walk up Ludgate Hill towards St Paul's Cathedral, a relatively insignificant street leads you to the Central Criminal Court, generally referred to as the Old Bailey. The court building dates from the early 20th century. The dome is topped with the statue of Justice, standing blindfolded with the scales of justice in her left hand and the sword of truth in her right. Major criminal cases are sent for trial at the Old Bailey by other courts in England and Wales.

CANNON STREET
STATION (below)

Two stone towers that used to stand at the entrance to the train-shed are all that remain of the original Cannon Street Station, completed in 1867. The white 1980s office blocks obscure most of the station when seen from above. This is a very busy commuter station during the working week, but virtually deserted at the weekend.

The formal green park on the river side of the station is in fact a roof garden, a lovely example of a green roof with trees and shrubs.

The South Bank

London "south of the river" has a somewhat separate identity from the capital's older areas to the north. For centuries the river served to isolate the marshy land to the south. When industry arrived in the 18th century, developers took advantage of the cheap land, river access and plenty of fresh water to build factories and warehouses. New bridges across the river and the emergence of the railways made the area accessible. Green fields gave way to factories and low-cost housing as the population increased dramatically.

Much of the South Bank was bombed-out during the Second World War. Ironically this devastation inspired the wholesale redevelopment of the riverside in the post-war years, and this is now one of London's most dynamic districts.

City Hall and the Scoop open space *left* and County Hall on the South Bank *above*

SOUTH BANK AND THE CITY

This view of the Thames as it flows through the centre of London brings an appreciation of how, as in centuries past, the capital's political, cultural and financial centres are still relatively close to each other.

The north bank is dominated by the legal and financial sector. The "Gherkin", Norman Foster's Swiss Re building and its more angular predecessor Tower 42 loom over the surrounding financial district.

Heading south across Waterloo Bridge, you pass the gaunt concrete South Bank Centre on the near side and the National Theatre on the far side before reaching the giant circular IMAX cinema and Waterloo Station. Trains and pedestrians cross from Charing Cross Station (seen here in the foreground) and the Embankment via the Hungerford train and pedestrian bridges.

The South Bank can be explored by the Jubilee Walkway, a riverside path that takes you from the London Aquarium and Jubilee Gardens past the South Bank arts complex, to the Tate Modern, Globe Theatre and Southwark Cathedral before turning north over Tower Bridge.

SOUTH BANK PANORAMA

The South Bank appears like a geometric sampler. Looking from right to left in this picture, the perfect circle of the London Eye is followed by the angular roofing of Waterloo Station, the reflex angle formed by the apartment block with the curved green copper roof of the Royal Festival Hall. Next door the Hayward Gallery in all its stark 1960s "brutalist" reinforced concrete, and so on past Waterloo Bridge to the slightly less confrontational buildings of the National Theatre.

This whole area suffered much bomb damage during the Second World War and its regeneration started with the 1951 Festival of Britain. The modernist Royal Festival Hall was built for the festival and was joined over the next 25 years by the National Film Theatre, the National Theatre and the Hayward Gallery. They are collectively known as the South Bank Centre. Raised pedestrian walkways on several levels characterise this cultural centre – and often bewilder visitors.

CITY HALL

The influence of Norman Foster on the contemporary London skyline cannot be ignored. The glass globe of City Hall, opened near Tower Bridge in 2002, is 148ft (45m) high. The architect based it on a modified sphere, creating 25 per cent less surface area than a more traditional rectangular shape. The sphere tilts back towards the south, and the floors step progressively inwards from top to bottom, providing its own shade and minimising the surface exposed to direct sunlight. This is the home of the London Assembly, the Greater London Authority and the office of the Mayor of London.

SOUTHWARK CATHEDRAL *(left)*

As the railway crosses the Thames from Cannon Street, the line cuts a swathe through the crowded environs of Southwark Cathedral. Much of the cathedral dates from 1220-1420. The road leading off London Bridge merges with Borough High Street, which runs through the borough of Southwark. This bohemian area is often simply known as The Borough.

GUY'S HOSPITAL AND LONDON BRIDGE STATION

Thomas Guy MP founded Guy's Hospital in 1721 for the treatment of incurables. Today this is a large teaching hospital which, in partnership with St Thomas' Hospital near Westminster Bridge, is one of the largest employers in the area.

Guy's backs onto London's oldest railway station, London Bridge. Part of the station is a terminus for routes from south London and Sussex, while through trains travel on to Cannon Street or Waterloo and Charing Cross.

TATE MODERN

Stride south across the Millennium Bridge and you arrive at the Tate Modern. Tate Britain's offspring occupies the shell of the old Bankside power station. The 325ft (99m) Bankside chimney was deliberately constructed to be lower than the dome of St Paul's Cathedral.

Two new storeys of glass known as the "lightbeam" were inserted along the full length of the building during the museum's conversion between 1998 and 2000. As a result visitors can view works displayed on the upper floors by natural light and enjoy dramatic views across London from the café.

Some installations remain the subject of controversy for months after opening, such as *The Weather Project* in 2003-4 in which Olafur Eliasson created shifting representations of the sun and sky with a tangible mist inside the huge Turbine Hall.

GLOBE THEATRE

When the American film director Sam Wanamaker came to London in 1949 he expected to find a fine monument to William Shakespeare. He was so disappointed that he began to plan and campaign for a replica of the Globe Theatre to be built. His determination won through and the circular thatched theatre we now see was completed in 1997. The building mirrors Shakespeare's original as closely as modern regulations would allow, using handmade bricks, oak laths, lime putty and plaster, and Norfolk water reed for the roof.

Every year from May to October the season of Shakespeare plays are acted out on the Tudor stage, while the audience sits in the galleries under eaves or stands in the central yard, open to the elements.

MILLENNIUM BRIDGE

Rising just 43ft (13m) above the Thames, this deceptively simple design won a competition organised by the Financial Times, the London Borough of Southwark and the Royal Institute of British Architects. The combined talents of the sculptor Sir Anthony Caro, the architect Sir Norman Foster and the engineer Ove Arup created an elegant suspension footbridge with its supporting cables dipping below eye-level to give unrestricted views of London.

LONDON EYE

Just as the Eiffel Tower in Paris outlived its original allotted lifespan to become an icon in its own right, so the London Eye seems set to become a permanent fixture on the London skyline. It opened in March 2000, with a five-year licence that has since been extended for a further 24 years.

The largest observation wheel ever built, it dwarfs Vienna's *Riesenrad*: it is 443ft (135m) across, and takes half an hour to turn a full revolution. On a clear day, at the top of the cycle you can see 25 miles (40km) right across London and beyond. Conversely its delicate outline is clearly visible from the surrounding hills at Richmond Park, Hampstead Heath and Crystal Palace.

After a couple of false starts, this 1,700 tonne Ferris wheel was successfully inched into position above the Thames over several days in October 1999. The giant A-frame legs that anchor the wheel's spindle stand in Jubilee Gardens and 80 fine cable spokes attach the hub and spindle to the rims of the wheel, which turns slowly above the river.

The 32 passenger capsules on the rim of the wheel can each carry 25 passengers. The wheel turns continuously at 10 inches (26cm) a second.

This was such a huge project that a single company could not make all the parts: the main frame was built in the Netherlands, the hub and spindle in the Czech Republic, the bearings in Germany, cables in Italy and capsules in France. It was assembled on the spot, on a temporary platform on the water.

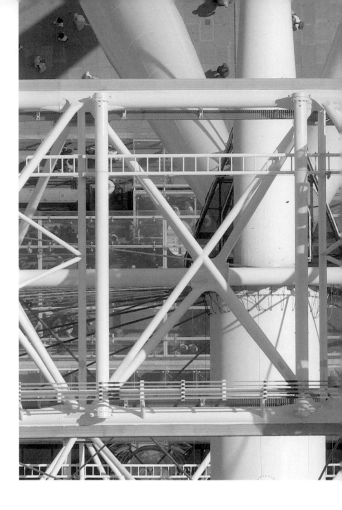

WATERLOO MILLENNIUM PIER

Beneath the London Eye riverboats call in at the Waterloo Millennium Pier on their way from Westminster to Greenwich, taking tourists on sightseeing cruises. In the picture below, the Jubilee Walkway passes in front of the elegant colonnades of County Hall and the pleasant parkland of Jubilee Gardens, created in 1977 to mark the silver jubilee of Elizabeth II. Walkers continue on to the Royal Festival Hall, the Oxo Tower and under Blackfriars Bridge to Tate Modern.

Behind the London Eye *(below left)* is Charing Cross station on the northern side of the Thames, together with the Hungerford railway and pedestrian bridges.

SOUTH BANK CENTRE

When the Festival of Britain was devised to raise the spirits of post-war Britain, this area was transformed from a scene of bombed-out devastation to a site of national celebration. While the Royal Festival Hall with its green copper roof is the only building that survives from the 1951 festival, the ethos remains and this has become a cultural centre for London. The concert hall is high in the building, to minimise the vibrations and noise of the nearby railway and roads.

In 1958 the National Film Theatre opened; it now hosts the London Film Festival every November. The harsh concrete blocks of the Hayward Gallery opened 10 years later to howls of dismay; however, few dispute that the displays inside present a dynamic range of contemporary and classical art. Sir Laurence Olivier's National Theatre Company finally found a permanent home at the National Theatre, which opened on the other side of Waterloo Bridge in 1976.

COUNTY HALL

Fierce political battles raged in the 1980s between the Labour-run Greater London Council and the Conservative Prime Minister Margaret Thatcher. County Hall was the council's base, an Edwardian baroque building right on the riverfront, opposite the Houses of Parliament. That war was won by Mrs Thatcher, who succeeded in abolishing the GLC. County Hall is now a mixture of hotel, private apartments and tourist attractions such as the London Aquarium and the Dali Universe.

Just before building of County Hall began in 1911, part of a Roman ship dating from about 300AD was discovered here. Sadly much of the find disintegrated but some timbers can still be seen at the Museum of London on London Wall.

BFI LONDON IMAX CINEMA

As traffic leaves the southern end of Waterloo Bridge, it enters a roundabout with the 10-storey IMAX cinema set in its depths. This huge glass drum, set on springs to counteract the traffic vibrations, houses Britain's largest cinema screen; its walls are decorated with a mural by the British artist Howard Hodgkin. Customers reach the IMAX on foot by the maze of underground passages that link Waterloo Station with the South Bank Centre and Waterloo Bridge.

Behind are the railway lines that run into Waterloo East and the Victory Arch, an imposing memorial to the dead of the two world wars, through which passengers enter the main Waterloo station.

HUNGERFORD BRIDGE

The brick piers that Isambard Kingdom Brunel built in 1845 to support his footbridge across the Thames survived the adaptation in 1864 which made Hungerford Bridge the only bridge in London to combine a rail and pedestrian crossing. In 2000 two new elegant suspension footbridges were erected either side of the main bridge that still carries trains from Charing Cross Station across the river.

WATERLOO STATION

In the second half of the 19th century a cluster of railway stations were built here, including the curiously named Necropolis station. Daily funerary trains left for Brookwood Cemetery near Guildford: the one-way ticket for the coffin cost 2s 6d.

Today's mainline station has 19 platforms for trains heading south-west to suburban London and the coast. Neighbouring Waterloo East is on the line out of Charing Cross station, serving south London and the south-east of England.

In 1994 the mainline station was extended to incorporate the two-level Eurostar terminal offering direct services to continental Europe. The 18-coach trains pull in to extra-long platforms under a dramatic 1,312ft (400m) long glass canopy.

Some people point to the irony that Waterloo, named after the battle in which Napoleon was defeated, welcomes trains from Belgium and France. A French politician tried unsuccessfully in 1998 to persuade the British Prime Minister to change its name. In 2007, however, all Eurostar services will move to the new terminal at St Pancras.

LAMBETH PALACE

Just across from the Houses of Parliament stands Lambeth Palace, owned by the Archbishops of Canterbury for 800 years. The early Archbishops would have arrived by water. Some etymologists say that the name Lambeth means "muddy landing place": when the first buildings were started, Lambeth Marsh stretched from here to Blackfriars.

The crypt and chapel date from the 13th century. The red-brick gatehouse is Tudor and the remarkable Great Hall was rebuilt with a hammerbeam roof in 1663, after the depredations of Cromwell's troops. Since 1829 the Great Hall has housed one of the oldest public libraries in the UK. Every 10 years or so the Archbishop of Canterbury convenes the Lambeth Conference, a consultative session with Anglican bishops from around the world.

VAUXHALL CROSS

Universally known to outsiders as the MI6 Building, this high-tech fortress on the Albert Embankment is the home of the Secret Intelligence Service. As the Foreign and Commonwealth Office puts it, SIS is "a Crown Service responsible for obtaining secret information and conducting operations in support of the UK's foreign policy objectives, and to counter threats to UK interests worldwide". With their emphasis on secrecy it is of course no surprise that the department's best-known operative, James Bond, is fictional. Insiders are more likely to refer to the building as "Legoland". Much of the 10-storey structure is below ground, walls and windows are bomb- and bullet-proof while rumour has it that wire mesh prevents interception of electronic messaging.

THE ELEPHANT AND CASTLE

Two large roundabouts and six major roads dominate this busy area of inner London, barely a mile south-east of Waterloo. A pub called the Elephant and Castle was listed here in the 1760s, and today the junction and the surrounding area of Newington are mostly known as the "Elephant". A 10-year programme of rebuilding was agreed in 2004 to include housing improvements, regeneration of the shopping areas and a new civic square.

IMPERIAL WAR MUSEUM

King George V opened the Imperial War Museum in 1920 as a memorial to those who had died or suffered during the First World War. It moved to Lambeth Road in 1936, occupying the former home of the Bethlem Royal Hospital (Bedlam). In recent decades it has expanded to encompass all aspects of modern warfare and conflicts, particularly those involving British or Commonwealth troops. The museum also administers collections at the Cabinet War Rooms in Whitehall, HMS *Belfast* in the Pool of London and Duxford Airfield near Cambridge.

THE OVAL

Every summer the Oval cricket ground in Kennington hosts the last Test match of the season. The ground's oval shape was determined long before it became a cricket venue – the road simply followed the shape of the original market garden. In 1846 Montpelier Cricket Club leased the ground from the Duchy of Cornwall and turfed it with grass cut from Tooting Common. In time the cricket club became the Surrey Cricket Club (the tenants to this day) and the Oval is seen as the home of County Cricket. Construction of the new OCS stand at the Vauxhall end of the ground was given the go-ahead in the teeth of local opposition and the stand opened in 2005.

In the early days the Oval also hosted significant football matches: in 1872 the first FA Cup final was played here (the Wanderers beat the Royal Engineers 1-0) and the following year England recorded their first international win, 4-2 against Scotland.

BATTERSEA POWER STATION

In the 44 years that Battersea Power Station was generating electricity (1939-83), opinion about the building shifted from "eyesore" to "heritage site". The original Station A's art deco interior ensured that the complex gained Grade II listed status.

Pop culture took the building to its heart when the band Pink Floyd designed the cover for their album *Animals* with a giant inflatable pink pig floating above the power station. In fact, the album picture had to be faked as the pig broke free from its moorings and floated away before a usable photo had been taken. A 1980s project to build a theme park on the site got no further than hoisting the giant generators out through the roof. In 2005 outline planning permission was granted to turn the site into an enormous entertainment and shopping complex.

NEW COVENT GARDEN MARKET

When you compare the area of the flower, fruit and vegetable wholesale market at Nine Elms with its old site three miles away at Covent Garden in central London, it is clear why the traders had to move out 30 years ago. The new site covers 56 acres (22.7 ha) on either side of the main railway line into Waterloo and 250 companies trade here. The working day starts at 3am, and is wrapped up by 11am. The fluorescent roof of the Flower Market is made of glass-reinforced polyester to give maximum natural light. The Fruit and Vegetable Market boasts 160 varieties of fruit and 180 different types of vegetables.

Docklands

The familiar loop of the River Thames' detour from Limehouse Reach to North Greenwich rounds the peninsula known as the Isle of Dogs. From the early 1800s the docks and shipyards in this area were busy with imports and exports until their closure in 1969 with the rise of container shipping. In the 1980s the commercial rebirth of Docklands began, transforming this long-neglected part of London. The resulting building boom produced a high-tech, high-rise business sector, a concrete jungle that defies the relative serenity of the surrounding waterways and the World Heritage Site of Greenwich and the Old Royal Naval College on the south bank. The 30-plus acres (12ha) of greenery in Mudchute are a happy legacy of the huge excavations of Millwall Docks in 1868.

The Isle of Dogs *left* and the Millennium Dome at Greenwich *above*

CANARY WHARF (left)

Two of London's most controversial buildings dominate the photograph. In the foreground, the stainless-steel tower with its pyramid-shaped roof is formally known as 1 Canada Square, but most Londoners simply call it Canary Wharf. London's tallest building, its defining shape can be seen for miles. Looking east across the Thames on the Blackwall Peninsula, the Millennium Dome is clearly visible, centre of furious political debate, and loved and scorned in equal measure by the British population.

From the west you approach the Isle of Dogs (top) via Limehouse Reach. On the south side of the river, street-names such as Shipwright Road and South Sea Street reflect the area's history. The *Mayflower* set out from Rotherhithe to America in 1620. The modern buildings of Bacon's College look out over Stave Hill ecological park and the Russia Dock woodland.

WEST INDIA DOCK

Some argue that these "immense air-conditioned filing cabinets" are symptoms of what architecture critics call lumpen skyscraper syndrome. Others point to the regeneration of an area that was in steep economic decline after the closure of the surrounding docks. It is clear that the high-density office buildings that now occupy the West India Docks and the advent of the Docklands Light Railway have had an irrevocable impact. Tenants of the towers include the *Daily Telegraph*, HSBC and Citigroup. Here and there some small touches soften the edges, such as the installation of a dozen nesting boxes for swifts high up on 1 Canada Square.

WESTFERRY ROAD

Running south from Westferry Docklands Light Railway (DLR) station, Westferry Road skirts the western perimeter of Docklands. From 1812-1844, a horse ferry operated between the Isle of Dogs and Greenwich, and this was one of the toll roads built to service the ferry.

The original wet docks were very much a closed area. To prevent thieves entering from the river, the area was walled off and only employees of the docks and Customs officials were allowed inside. The West India Dock Company employed its own police force to keep people out.

Most of the modern buildings between Canada Square and Westferry Circus are built on "water platforms", standing on piles driven into the riverbed and suspended above the water. However those to the east of Canada Square are built as "holes in the water" with basement parking and services. The concentric circles of Westferry Circus offer a shaded promenade for office workers.

CANARY WHARF STATION (right)

At the heart of the Canary Wharf office and shopping complex is the Canary Wharf DLR station. Its distinctive curved glass roof shelters six platforms where the automated trains pull in. The DLR was built specifically to service this area, running from Tower Gateway and Bank in the City of London. Much of this line is elevated. Extensions now serve Lewisham in the south, Beckton in the east and Stratford in the north.

LONDON ARENA

On the quayside of Millwall Inner Dock, the London Arena was built on the site of an old tomato and banana warehouse that belonged to the shipping company Fred Olsen. It was refurbished in 1999, 10 years after it opened, so that its capacity could be altered hydraulically from 500 to 12,500 spectators. However by 2004 there were no more sporting events, pop concerts or trade shows and the Arena's future, closely linked with that of the Millennium Dome, was uncertain.

WHITECHAPEL

The East London Mosque on Whitechapel Road is one of Britain's largest, with room for more than 3,000 worshippers in one sitting. On holy days such as Eid as many as 15,000 people will come to the mosque. Four times a day the call to prayer echoes from the minaret around the neighbouring streets. Muslims are one of London's largest religious communities today.

The area around Whitechapel Road and Brick Lane is known locally as Banglatown, as many of the locals are of Bangladeshi origin. People come from all over London to the buzzing street market on Brick Lane.

Britain's oldest manufacturing company, the Whitechapel Bell Foundry, is still in business here. It was founded during the reign of Elizabeth I. All sorts of bells, from hand bells to giant church bells, are cast in its workshop. Perhaps its most famous bell is Big Ben (over 13 tonnes) which hangs in the Clock Tower of the Palace of Westminster.

Shadwell Basin (right) is all that remains of the mighty London Docks which once covered over 30 acres of the northern bank of the Thames between Wapping and Tower Bridge. The water is now used for canoeing and watersports and stylish new apartment blocks line the banks.

LIMEKILN DOCK, LIMEHOUSE

The new flats on Dundee Wharf beside Limekiln Dock are at the heart of Limehouse, an area to the east of Wapping that used to be considered London's Chinatown. Production of quick lime for building mortar in Limekiln Dock during the 14th century gave the district its name. The diarist Samuel Pepys recorded visiting a porcelain factory here in 1660.

In 1901 you could sail from Dundee Wharf on one of four large steamships owned by the Dundee Perth and London Shipping Company on regular twice-weekly sailings between London and Dundee. A century later after two world wars and the slump in shipping, the docks are no more, the ships are gone and a new footbridge curves across Limekiln Dock, between the smart apartment blocks.

EXCEL LONDON

From the London Boat Show, the British International Motor Show to arms fairs and travel trade exhibitions, companies of all sorts display their wares every year at this ultra modern exhibition centre just three minutes from London City Airport. The ExCeL centre, built on the site of the Royal Victoria Dock, was opened in 2000.

MILLENNIUM DOME

The largest single-roofed structure in the world, 1,198ft (365m) across with twelve 328ft (100m) steel masts, the Millennium Dome was built to mark the turn of the millennium. It was originally designed as a focal point for national celebrations but the spectacular structure was dogged by political controversy from the beginning. Richard Rogers' bold circular dome was never matched by the exhibition inside, which was originally intended to be a portrait of the nation. The Dome remained in the public eye for all the wrong reasons, as the media highlighted the huge cost (£770m) to the taxpayer and the 50 per cent shortfall in visitor numbers which totalled just over six million by December 31 2000, when it closed. Its future was increasingly uncertain – there were stalled proposals to turn it into a business park or a giant casino. In May 2005 the American-based Anschutz Entertainment Group and British mobile phone company O2 announced plans to re-launch the Dome as an entertainments and sports complex, including a 2,000-capacity ice rink.

CITY AIRPORT

The defunct Royal Albert Dock was born again as London City Airport in 1985, with commercial flights lifting off from a short runway. Seven years later the runway was extended and by 2000 more than 1.5m passengers were using the airport every year.

A privately-owned airport at the heart of London's Docklands, City Airport is proud to be small. It boasts check-in times of just 10 minutes, and even shorter times to reunite passengers with their suitcases on arrival. Passengers are predominantly business travellers en route to mainland Europe (Belgium, France, Germany, Italy, Luxembourg, Netherlands, Switzerland), destinations in the UK and Ireland.

Every July the airport hosts a fun day out for families raising money for a local hospice. Events include an air show, funfair and arts and crafts displays.

ROYAL VICTORIA DOCK, SILVERTOWN

Immediately to the west of London City Airport is the Royal Victoria Dock. London's first steamship dock, it opened in 1855. It was designed to accommodate the increasingly large cargo ships, up to 8000 tonnes. The original layout had nearly three miles of quays along five "finger" jetties, each 580ft (177m) long. There were specialist storage houses for fruit such as oranges and bananas (the Banana Berth had great mechanical buckets to move the fruit from the boat) and meat from South America. Bonded warehouses were built for the giant half-tonne barrels or "hogsheads" of American tobacco. Since the dock closed in 1981, the ExCeL exhibition centre has sprung up and plans are afoot to build a giant aquarium on the southern quay.

WOOLWICH FERRY

Drivers on the busy North Circular and South Circular roads in East London can take the Woolwich Ferry when they need to cross the river. Three boats operate on this free service for cars and pedestrians between North Woolwich pier just off the Albert Road in Silvertown and Woolwich proper on the southern side of the Thames. The trip takes just 15 minutes – five to get on, five across and five to unload.

THAMES BARRIER *(right)*

The Thames is tidal from the estuary through London to Teddington, west of Richmond. Records show that high water levels have risen significantly at London Bridge over the past 100 years. The capital has always been at risk of floods when surge tides in the North Atlantic combine with north winds to force vast amounts of water up the Thames. In 1983 the Thames Tidal Barrier, a triumph of engineering about a mile upstream from the Woolwich Ferry, was completed and raised for the first time. The huge steel piers are linked to moveable gates that are raised from the riverbed to hold back the waters when they threaten London.

LOWER THAMES

As the river passes the Millennium Dome at Greenwich and heads down from London towards the sea, it makes several dramatic loops that give stunning views across the capital. Travel down the river from Richmond to the Thames Barrier and much of London past and present is encapsulated on its shores: the power of medieval bishops at Lambeth; politics ancient and modern at the Palace of Westminster; commerce and tradition in the City of London; the lost legacy of the docks transformed into dynamic centres for modern businesses in Docklands.

While the river's importance as a transport route has declined dramatically in the past century, it remains a place of work for some, with barges transporting heavy goods, river buses and cruise boats. River trade may yet see an increase, as transporting non-perishable goods by water is considerably more environmentally-friendly than the road haulage culture of the early 21st century.

The Suburbs

FROM THE AIR much of suburbia seems to blend into one continuous mass, but on the ground each "London village" has its own distinct characteristic. Leafy Richmond's Georgian villas, Roehampton's modernist high-rise blocks, Ilford's earnest rows of terraced houses and Southall's Asian shopping centre all contrast with that ultimate experiment in suburban living, Hampstead Garden Suburb. The social reformer Henrietta Barnet sought to avoid building another suburb with "rows of ugly villas such as disfigure Willesden and most of the suburbs of London". Working with the architect and planner Raymond Unwin, her vision of wide tree-lined roads, each house with its own garden, remains largely in place today. Rather less so her vision of HGS as a place for "persons of all classes of society and standards of income" – 100 years later, the Suburb is resoundingly middle class.

Windsor and its castle *right* contrast with terraced houses in Ilford *above*

HAMPTON COURT (left)

During the reign of Henry VIII, Hampton Court became one of Europe's most lavish palaces. Much of what we see today is the original Tudor palace that survived the best efforts of Sir Christopher Wren to persuade William III to raze it to the ground. The intricate pattern of the Privy Garden was recently restored to the design that William III would have known. Behind the palace are the Wilderness Gardens and the famous maze that dates from 1691.

WINDSOR CASTLE

When the Royal Standard flies from the Round Tower, the Queen is in residence. Elizabeth II regularly spends a month here at Easter, and a week in June when she travels through Windsor Great Park to watch the Royal Ascot races.

Windsor is the world's largest occupied castle. For over 900 years, it has been a fortress during times of war and palatial royal residence in times of peace. William I laid the first foundations here to protect his newly acquired capital, London, just a day's march further east. Eight hundred years later Windsor Castle was one of Queen Victoria's favourite homes. Prince Albert died of typhoid in the castle in 1861.

In modern times Windsor has often been the setting for State visits by foreign dignitaries, who arrive with all the traditional pomp of horse-drawn carriages.

The Thames at Richmond

It is unusual for a view to be protected by an Act of Parliament, but then this view was immortalised by artists such as JMW Turner. When developers proposed building on Petersham Meadows at the start of the 20th century, artists, residents and conservationists campaigned successfully for the land on and below Richmond Hill to be preserved.

Cattle graze the meadows here in the summer months as they have for centuries. At the top of the hill stands the Royal Star and Garter Home, founded in 1916 for the care of ex-servicemen and women.

Richmond and its neighbours Ham, Petersham and Twickenham are rich in parkland. Deer still roam the 2,500 acres (25,000ha) of Richmond Park, first enclosed by Charles I. On the other side of the river are the gardens of Marble Hill House, which George II built for his mistress, Henrietta Howard.

The Thames winds from Hampton Court past Ham House, Marble Hill and Glover's Island then continues under Richmond Bridge (the oldest bridge on the river) towards Kew.

National Archives

Known as the Public Records Office until it merged with the Historical Manuscripts Commission in April 2003, the huge collection at the National Archives at Kew allows public access to all the records of central government and the law courts in the United Kingdom, from the 11th century to the present. Inevitably the nearby superstores of Kew retail park draw rather more visitors.

KEW GARDENS

The Royal Botanic Gardens at Kew was the brainchild of George III's mother Augusta, who lived at Kew Palace. George commissioned the octagonal Great Pagoda, one of a series of follies, which was built in 1762. Today's extraordinary botanical collection (more than 38,000 plant species) was founded on specimens collected by the keeper, Sir Joseph Banks, as he travelled the world in the late 18th century. A Chilean wine palm brought to Kew as a seed in 1846 still grows in the Temperate House which, together with the huge Palm House, was built in the mid 19th century to enable plants to be kept at temperatures and humidity levels that closely mirrored their native climates. The Princess of Wales Conservatory was opened in 1987 in memory of Princess Augusta: a dramatic building with angular, stepped roofs that slope down to the ground and much of its display space below ground level.

CLAPHAM JUNCTION

Who was "the man on the Clapham omnibus"? A law lord, Lord Bowen coined the phrase in 1903 to indicate an ordinary person who is reasonably well educated, but not a specialist in the subject under discussion. Today's judges should perhaps turn to the commuters at Clapham Junction railway station, as it is Britain's busiest, with some 2,500 trains a day passing through its 16 platforms.

Before the era of rail travel began Battersea, where the station is located, was largely working-class and its main claim to fame was the lavender that grew locally. Clapham was a mile away and much more genteel: it seems when the station was opened in 1863 the railway companies aspired to attract more middle-class passengers and named it accordingly.

CROYDON AIRPORT

Croydon Aerodrome, as it was known when it opened in 1920, was London's first official airport. Imperial Airways ran regular scheduled passenger flights to Paris, Amsterdam and Rotterdam and by 1923 you could also fly to Berlin. Air travel was glamorous and exciting – Croydon saw the arrival of Charles Lindbergh in 1927 after he flew solo across the Atlantic for the first time. Amy Johnson was the first woman to fly from Croydon to Australia.

After playing a crucial role during the Second World War, Croydon Airport resumed civilian flights. During the 1950s it became clear there was no room for expansion and Heathrow was earmarked as London's airport. Croydon closed in 1959; some of the terminal buildings remain.

CRYSTAL PALACE

The great steel and glass structure that was Crystal Palace started its life in Hyde Park as the centrepiece of Prince Albert's Great Exhibition of 1851, a showcase of everything that he considered made Britain great. After the exhibition, its designer Sir Joseph Paxton found backers to buy the building and move it south to Sydenham Hill, surrounding it with a beautiful park with fountains and temples. A disastrous fire in 1936 destroyed the glasshouse; today little remains except the park and some statuary.

John Logie Baird, the Scottish television pioneer, rented studios in Crystal Palace in the 1930s. Today the BBC transmitter stands proud amid the Victorian terraces.

WIMBLEDON

The All England Croquet Club was so enthused about the new game of lawn tennis (or "sphairistike") when it was introduced in 1875, that in two years the club had changed its name to the All England Lawn Tennis and Croquet Club. The men's singles championship started in 1877, the women's in 1884 and, in 1905, an American woman was the first overseas player to win here. Today Wimbledon is the only Grand Slam tournament still played on grass.

ATHLETICS AT CRYSTAL PALACE

The National Sports Centre at Crystal Palace was built in the 1960s. While the indoor sports centre and stadium has been the scene of many record-breaking national and international competitions (and it still hosts the annual athletics Grand Prix) the building is now dated and a new sports facility is planned for 2009.

Downhill from the sports centre is the boating lake; clustered around its shores are the famous model dinosaurs much as the Victorians would have seen them 150 years ago.

OLD ROYAL NAVAL COLLEGE, GREENWICH

Seen from the Thames, the Old Royal Naval College at Greenwich is quite simply breathtaking. At the end of the 17th century, Sir Christopher Wren designed this magnificent baroque setpiece, with its immaculately landscaped gardens, as Greenwich Hospital for the care of seamen and their families. From 1875 to 1998 it served as the Royal Naval College for the training of naval officers. Today, three of the buildings house the University of Greenwich and the fourth is home to the Trinity College of Music.

A little further upstream, Greenwich Pier is a popular point to pick up a river cruise. Nearby the famous tea-clipper *Cutty Sark*, one of the fastest ships of her day, sits in dry dock.

ROYAL OBSERVATORY, GREENWICH

Charles II built the observatory in 1675 for his Astronomer Royal to work on improving navigation at sea. The challenge was to devise a means of calculating a ship's exact position when out of sight of land: in 1773 John Harrison, a clockmaker, succeeded. The prime meridian, 0° longitude, passes through the observatory: all distances east or west are measured from this notional line.

ALEXANDRA PALACE

Known as the People's Palace, the original exhibition and recreation centre at Alexandra Palace near Muswell Hill opened in 1873 to widespread acclaim, but 16 days later it went up in flames. It was quickly rebuilt and for over 130 years "Ally-Pally", with its indoor ice-rink and landscaped gardens has been a popular attraction for north Londoners.

This was the birthplace of the BBC's television services and served from 1936-1956 as the main TV transmitting centre, with regular concerts and live shows. News bulletins continued to be produced here after that. Today the antenna mast can still be seen for miles around, mirroring that of Crystal Palace to the south.

Muswell Hill itself was seen as rather sedate in the 1950s. Today it has been transformed into a trendy village, popular with theatre and media professionals and those who commute into central London.

EDMONTON CEMETERY

A reminder of the Victorian era, when the railway came to Lower Edmonton in the 1870s. Working-class families flocked to Edmonton as workmen's fares for early morning trains into the City were remarkably cheap. Edmonton today mixes Victorian workers' cottages with 1960s tower blocks.

HAMPSTEAD PONDS

Separating the upmarket villages of Hampstead and Highgate is Hampstead Heath. It is home to Kenwood House with its lakeside concerts in the summer, Parliament Hill and its lovely views over London and the famous Hampstead bathing ponds where hardy swimmers break the ice in the middle of winter to be sure of their daily dip.

TWICKENHAM STADIUM

What Wembley is to football, Twickenham is to rugby (union, that is). On match days the crowds stream towards the stadium and help explain why the town has a remarkably large number of pubs and restaurants. Occasionally it is hired out for other events. Recent years have seen concerts by the Rolling Stones, who used to play at Twickenham's Eel Pie Island hotel during the 1960s. The stadium was rebuilt during the 1990s and now incorporates the Museum of Rugby. Here you can see trophies including the Calcutta Cup, which is a legacy of Britain's colonial past. Two hundred and seventy silver rupees were melted down to make the cup, which has been awarded every year since 1879 to the winners of a match between England and Scotland.

WEMBLEY STADIUM

The iconic twin towers of the old stadium are gone, mourned by many football fans who gloried in the memories of England's win in the 1966 World Cup final and other sporting triumphs at Wembley. The stadium's developers are hoping that the new giant arch will gain much the same place in their affections. It is certainly visible right across London. The 436ft (133m) tall arch is not just aesthetically pleasing: it serves to support the retractable roof, a clever design that ensures no pillars obscure the view of the 90,000 spectators, whether they are here for football, athletics or concerts. The Millennium Stadium in Cardiff assumed Wembley's role as the national stadium during the rebuild. Only time will tell whether Wembley will once more become the UK's favourite.

HEATHROW AIRPORT

When the first BOAC flight arrived from Australia at the Heath Row Airport in 1946, there were no terminal buildings, just a few tents. The first year of operation saw 900 flights in and out, and 60,000 passengers used the airport. By 2005 passenger numbers had risen to 67m, a fifth terminal was under construction, and there were 1,260 flights a day – or one flight every 90 seconds.

Airport and airlines alike are confident that the demand for air travel is insatiable and Heathrow's

Terminal 5, on the western side of the airport, will raise the airport's capacity to 90m passengers a year. When the main part, Concourse A, opens in 2008 it will have a 1,312ft (400m) long wave-shaped roof. Terminal 5 had a controversial start as local residents vehemently opposed an increase in Heathrow's capacity. They continue to argue that the greater noise and air pollution as well as increased traffic are too heavy a price to pay for being one of the world's leading airports.

DARTFORD CROSSING

The Queen Elizabeth II bridge is the most easterly point of the M25 London Orbital
Motorway. Officially opened by the Queen in October 1991 the bridge is used by
traffic travelling from Essex into Kent; northbound vehicles travelling anticlockwise
use the two Dartford tunnels bored under the river. It was the first bridge to be built
in an entirely new location on the river Thames for more than 50 years.